# My Sister and Me

# My Sister and Me

## *Poems and Rhymes*

*To Susan
love + Best Wishes —
Kelvin x*

### Kelvin Smith

Copyright © 2015 by Kelvin Smith.

ISBN:	Softcover	978-1-5144-6466-3
	eBook	978-1-5144-6465-6

All rights reserved. No part of this book may be reproduced or transmitted in any form or by any means, electronic or mechanical, including photocopying, recording, or by any information storage and retrieval system, without permission in writing from the copyright owner.

Any people depicted in stock imagery provided by Thinkstock are models, and such images are being used for illustrative purposes only.
Certain stock imagery © Thinkstock.

Print information available on the last page.

Rev. date: 11/11/2015

**To order additional copies of this book, contact:**
Xlibris
800-056-3182
www.Xlibrispublishing.co.uk
Orders@Xlibrispublishing.co.uk
719226

# CONTENTS

My Sister And Me ................................................................. 1
It's Not A Crime (*To Rhyme All The Time*) ........................ 2
Wimberry Mountain (*Penyrheol*) ...................................... 3
Same Old Thing .................................................................. 4
No Title ............................................................................... 5
Fairy Tales Made True ......................................................... 6
Chuckle Buckle .................................................................... 7
Someone's Missing This Christmas ...................................... 8
Oh To Be A Chambermaid (*When Julie Got The Job!*) ....... 9
Cruel To Be Kind ................................................................ 10
If The World Stopped Turning ............................................ 11
Lust Don't Last For Long .................................................... 12
Oh! To Have A Horse .......................................................... 13
If I Get To Heaven .............................................................. 14
Poo! ..................................................................................... 15
Where The Bluebells Grew .................................................. 16
One Fine Day ...................................................................... 17
Am I A Nutter? .................................................................... 18
I Know That Face ................................................................ 19
A Sperm's Destiny ............................................................... 20
More Content ...................................................................... 21
Mum Sent Me To ................................................................ 22
There's Unique …. They Called Me Goldie! ....................... 24
How Do The Australians? ….. (*Tell Me Liz!*) ..................... 25
Snore – Snore! ..................................................................... 26
She Cries ............................................................................. 27
Stick A Pin .......................................................................... 28
Chocolate Biscuits ............................................................... 29
Teddy On The Shelf ............................................................ 30
Promotion Swagger! ............................................................ 31

We Were Children In The Playground..................................32
Bethlehem By Dawn ........................................................34
I Used To But No More ....................................................35
The Gooney Bird..............................................................36
In Loving Memory Of Vaseline .........................................37
Fish Fingers......................................................................38
Best Say Goodbye.............................................................39
Faces ...............................................................................40
I've Been A Glutton!.........................................................41
Ice Blue Jeans And Records ..............................................42
Lilly May ........................................................................43
Page From A Book ...........................................................44
Obsessed With Stars.........................................................45
Scream (*Edvard Munch*) ..................................................46
Was .................................................................................47
Little Budgie ...................................................................48
My Willie.........................................................................49
No More Mummy............................................................50
Susan Swot......................................................................51
Well Dressed Man............................................................52
Silly Names .....................................................................53
A Visit To St. Martins ......................................................54
Silence Not Golden .........................................................55
Jingle Bloody Bells ...........................................................56
I Did Bring Your Flowers .................................................57
The Great Cheese Shortage...............................................58
Without Love...................................................................59
Blaa Blaa Bald Sheep .......................................................60
Love Me Always...............................................................61
Uncle Fred's Jumper.........................................................62
Strolling On A Moon ......................................................63
I'm Just A Snail ................................................................64
Sometimes.......................................................................65
If I Could Fly ..................................................................66
Turtle Soup .....................................................................67
Just Thinking ..................................................................68
Raining Animals..............................................................70

| | |
|---|---|
| Feelng Good | 71 |
| Dummy? | 72 |
| Letter From Hell | 73 |
| Poor Spider | 74 |
| Oranges Are Orange | 75 |
| Sit! | 76 |
| A Walk 'Round The Old Raspberry Pass | 77 |
| Boys? – Yuk! | 78 |
| You're Going Now | 79 |
| Parents Lie | 80 |
| Mr January Cold | 81 |
| The Dodo | 82 |
| Blue Hill (*Bryn Glas*) | 83 |
| Four Leaf Clover | 84 |
| Dad | 85 |
| British Toilet Weather | 86 |
| London Marathon (*Debbie's Wish*) | 87 |
| God Is | 88 |
| Do You Ever? | 89 |
| The Middle Of Somewhere | 90 |
| Dream You Life Away | 91 |
| Kangaroos In Kent? | 92 |
| Down By The Sea | 93 |
| Pearly Queens | 94 |
| Barbarella | 95 |
| Lost Kitten | 96 |
| Lovers' Day | 97 |
| Obvious | 98 |
| Not Flat? | 99 |
| Are We Nearly There Mam? | 100 |
| Toast My Birthday | 101 |
| Gavin The Pig | 102 |
| Cwtch (*Cuddle*) | 103 |
| Ponty Park | 104 |
| Alone At Night (*A Non Rhymer Professor!*) | 105 |
| What's The Crack Girls? | 106 |
| Across The Sea | 107 |

(*Aunty*) Queenie Got The Ball ............................................................. 108
A Weekend's Murder .............................................................................. 109
Fallen Cross ............................................................................................. 110
Oops (*A Man's Forgetfulness*) ............................................................... 111
Is Heaven In The Sun? ........................................................................... 112
Hypochondriac ....................................................................................... 113
A Few More Nursery Rhymes Revisited As A Kid ........................... 114
Short Love (*Written For Sister Hayley's Wedding*) ............................ 115
Peaceful Waters ...................................................................................... 116
In The Genes .......................................................................................... 117
School Dinner Money ........................................................................... 118
Pete The Peacock .................................................................................... 119
Tick–Tock ................................................................................................ 120
Joey Drakers ............................................................................................ 121
Happy Families? ..................................................................................... 122
Poor Mouse ............................................................................................. 123
You'll Soon Realise ................................................................................. 124
Angel ........................................................................................................ 125
Spotted Dick ........................................................................................... 126
My Questions ......................................................................................... 127
Always ...................................................................................................... 128
Reflection ................................................................................................ 129
Auntie Minnie ........................................................................................ 130
If Ever I Come Back .............................................................................. 131
Beggar? ..................................................................................................... 132
My Epitaph (*Or One Of Them!*) ........................................................ 133
Just Another Day ................................................................................... 134
Divorce .................................................................................................... 135
The Last Few Days Of A Sparrow ....................................................... 136
Absent Friends ....................................................................................... 137
A '99' Please ............................................................................................ 138
Jack And Bill .......................................................................................... 139
If Grandad Would Only Die (*His Favourite Poem!*) ....................... 140
More Honest .......................................................................................... 141
The Mole ................................................................................................. 142
Where Once The Green Grass Lay ..................................................... 143
Where's Jesus When You Need Him? ................................................. 144

I Fell ............................................................................................. 145
Don't It Make You Laugh? ........................................................ 146
Cease Your Hurt ......................................................................... 147
Our Sunny Special Day (*With Callum, Aged Two*) ..................... 148
60th Birthday Reflections .......................................................... 149
Creepy Crawly Spider ................................................................ 150
I Am Here ................................................................................... 151
Guts Full .................................................................................... 152
Under The Stars ......................................................................... 153
Joe ............................................................................................. 154
Palpitations ................................................................................ 155
Why? ......................................................................................... 156
Mr Choo .................................................................................... 157
Mother's Day .............................................................................. 158
The Owl's C.v. ............................................................................ 159
Millionaire ................................................................................. 160
No Matter .................................................................................. 161
If I Could .................................................................................. 162
Aunty Sandy .............................................................................. 163
Stardom Or Bust ........................................................................ 164
He's Waiting There .................................................................... 165
Skimble-Skamble ....................................................................... 166
Granny Smith ............................................................................ 167
Can't Do It On My Own ........................................................... 168
Crap Christmas .......................................................................... 169
Goodbye (*Outro*) ...................................................................... 170

I'd like to dedicate this Book to

**Mullac the Magician**

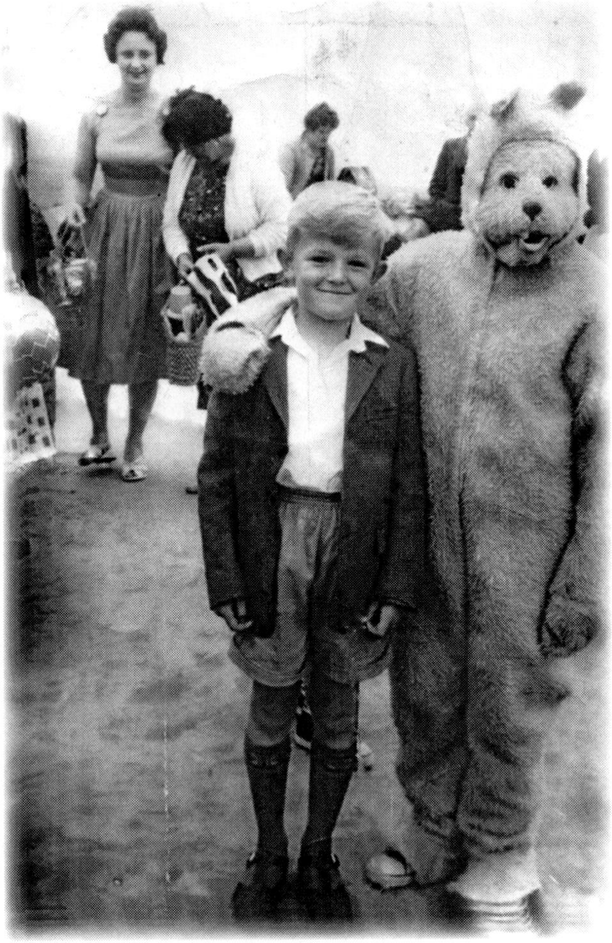

# MY SISTER AND ME
## (*On the photo alongside*)

My sister and me
Down by the sea,
I'm on the left -
She's taller than me.

She's quite protective
And as you can see,
She dressed to impress –
But quite oddly.

I got used to the point
And many a stare,
My sister and me
(Well me and the bear!)

I never found out
If she looks like me,
Or if she still does
Now she's over sixty.

We've had a good life
Though she's out of her tree,
(Me and the bear)
My sister and me.

Kelvin Smith

# IT'S NOT A CRIME
## *(To Rhyme all the Time)*

It's not a crime
To rhyme all the time
And now I'm mature enough,
To say that blank verse
Does make me curse
And I don't like that stuff.

And to those who compose
Free verse and prose
And others that always rhyme,
Let's all dare
To Scarborough Fair
Cause rhyming's a true friend of mine.

No rhyme or reason
Love or Treason
From my new dawn until it's bedtime,
Many a ditty
Serious or witty
I just can't help making it rhyme.

So dear assessor
Critique Professor
Remember it's not a crime,
It's hullabaloo
I do what I do
And that's rhyming all of the time.

# WIMBERRY MOUNTAIN
## (*Penyrheol*)

Yellow sun
Purple fun
Wimberries on the Hill,
Walk with kin
Purple skin
Stained by purple fill.

Mountain high
Touch the sky
Roll around the fern,
When I die
Here I'll lie
With the sun I'll burn.

Shadows fall
Homeward crawl
Sunset orange sky,
Once we're fed
Off to bed
Purple dragons fly.

*Kelvin Smith*

# SAME OLD THING

Up in the morning, what will today bring?
Well I'll tell you – the same old thing.
Off to work for the same old dime,
Leave the house the same old time.

The same old people on the same old train,
The same old dear with the same old pain.
The same old conversation, that's all I've heard,
From the same old guys doing the same crossword.

The same snogging couple (back seat together),
The same cool grandad in his same old leather.
The same old stubble on the same old chins,
The same bit of stuff flashing her same old pins.

The same ticket collector with his same old joke,
On the 8.30 train it's the same old folk.
Get to work and it's the same old jobs,
The same old filling in the tea break cobs.

The same way home – the same way in,
The same old house and overflowing bin.
The same old wife with the same old patter,
The same old hug and the same old chatter.

Same old food down the same old belly,
Same old programmes on the same old telly.
Same old position in the same old bed,
The same old grunt since they've been wed.

So whether you're a chef, a priest or a King,
Everyday it's the same old thing!

# NO TITLE

Her reflection in the mirror
Had feathers in her hair,
With a bloodless complexion
I couldn't help but stare.

I think she knew I ogled her
I prayed she wouldn't stray,
I walked closer to the mirror
But she never looked my way.

I felt hypnotized by her presence
I watched her stand so still,
She turned and then looked back again
I felt a sudden chill.

And then a crack! – the mirror split
It gave me such a scare,
I turned from her reflection
To find she wasn't there.

*Kelvin Smith*

# FAIRY TALES MADE TRUE

Yellow fields, blue woods and green hills,
Castle walls, babbling brooks and wind mills.

Floating clouds, dazzling sun and later auburn skies,
Birds fly home, so do we, with weary buttercup eyes.

Swaying trees, honey bees and miles of blackberry lanes,
Darkening skies, setting sun as homeland in our veins.

Turns of storytelling, all our summer through,
All with happy endings, that's our promise too.

Homeward bound, familiar sounds while holding hands with you,
Nursery rhymes, happy times and fairy tales made true.

*My Sister and Me*

# CHUCKLE BUCKLE

You only had those shoes today
Everyone was chuffed,
You just wait till mum sees them
Now that they're all scuffed.

I take size 4s
You take size 2s,
I wouldn't like to be –
In your shoes.

*Kelvin Smith*

# SOMEONE'S MISSING THIS CHRISTMAS

Someone's missing this Christmas
Someone's not at home,
Someone's cold this Christmas
On the streets they roam.

Someone's hurting this Christmas
Hurting for someone missing,
Someone needs holding this Christmas
Need loving – hugging – kissing.

Memories flood back this Christmas
To once when they were here,
Someone's alone this Christmas
And all through New Year.

Someone didn't celebrate Christmas
White Christmas turned out blue,
With unwrapped presents under the tree
Still waiting there for you.

# OH TO BE A CHAMBERMAID
## (When Julie got the Job!)

Oh to be a chambermaid
I cannot wait to see,
Myself in a short black dress and hold ups –
That's the life for me.

But then my dreams were shattered
My interview was a sham,
They said I didn't get the job –
Because I'm a frigging man!

# CRUEL TO BE KIND

Sat sipping tea on an Autumn day
While the wind howls outside,
My blanket keeps me nice and warm
With my best friend by my side.

She looks up at me time and again
I pat her on the head,
She's all I have in the world
So there'll be no more tears shed.

I sit here with my memories
As they make me laugh and sigh,
But I'm content to sit with her
Until my turn to die.

We've both grown old together
We wouldn't be without each other,
She is my little baby girl
Suppose I am her mother.

When it's time I'll take her too
Sounds cruel but it's kind,
She'll be safe and warm with me
I can't leave her behind.

We both sip tea on a Winter's day
Then leave the world outside,
My electric blanket will keep me warm
With my best friend wrapped inside.

*My Sister and Me*

# IF THE WORLD STOPPED TURNING

If the world stopped turning
And we got stuck on day,
We wouldn't be able to say goodnight –
What else could we say?

Because if you stop and think about it
There would be no more night,
So perhaps when we went up to bed –
We could all just say – good-light.

(so just in case, we're all ready now)

*Kelvin Smith*

# LUST DON'T LAST FOR LONG

Please don't flirt
Please don't hurt
The love they have inside,
Please don't stray
And walk away
And leave the tears they've cried.

Infatuations pass
Lust don't last,
Then what will you do?
Hold on and see
Because love's the key
As lust will hurt you too.

Now you're alone
To proud to phone
Your nights long and cold,
You're hurt instead
You've made your bed
No-one left to hold.

Search your heart
From the start
Hold on to being strong,
Please don't stray
And walk away
Lust don't last for long.

# OH! TO HAVE A HORSE

Oh! To have a horse
(We've all said that),
They always said they'd get me one
But I made do with a cat!

Oh to have a stable
And a horsey hat,
But I made do with a Wendy House
That housed that naughty cat.

My cat's name is Champion
Named after the wonder horse,
I've tried to teach her dressage
But it never works of course.

I rode my horse a few times
When I saddled my champion cat,
But I went and fell off time and again
(Well we've all done that).

Haven't we?

*Kelvin Smith*

# IF I GET TO HEAVEN

If I get to Heaven
I will look for you,
'Cause I am certain you'll be there
You're one of the few.

If you know I'm coming
Perhaps you'll look for me,
'Cause I will certainly look for you
I won't let you be.

So if I get to Heaven
So help me God willing,
I will spend my time with you
And my ever after will be fulfilling.

So if you know I'm coming
Please meet me at the gate,
'Cause I'll be waiting there for you
Like at hometime – I can't wait.

*My Sister and Me*

# POO!

When I get in, do you know what I'm going to do?
Straight to the toilet and have a poo!

I hate using toilets when I'm out and about,
So I'll wait till I get home there's no doubt.

Something we all have and that's the knack,
Of holding it in all the way back.

To get into my own toilet and sit on my own loo,
Is sheer bliss when I need a Poo!

*Kelvin Smith*

# WHERE THE BLUEBELLS GREW

There's a place I know
Where the bluebells grow.
In a wood off Bedwas Hill,
Where the sun shines through
Where I walked with you
And the place where I walk still.

When I smell the dew
Through the bluebells new
The scent just fills my head,
In this blue lush land
I can feel your hand
And hear the things you said.

Though we've pastures new
And new loved ones too
I can't help reminisce,
When I walked with you
Where the bluebells grew
We both stole our first kiss.

*My Sister and Me*

# ONE FINE DAY ......

One fine day I'm going to run away
To some far off distant shore,
Where bikini clad girls, dive for pearls
Down to the ocean floor.

Under a coconut tree sat by the sea
I'll sun my days away,
Till the tide comes in, I'll sip pink gin
And watch the dolphins play.

Then all to soon watch the rising moon
Light up paradise sky,
Then I'll fall asleep by the ocean deep
As a skein of geese glide by.

Then the very next day I'm going to run away
And do the same again,
Just for fun, I'll lie in the sun
Out of the South Wales rain.

Just imagine those sands running through our hands
In paradise far away,
Come and dream with me of that coconut tree
It'll brighten up our day.

So let's paddle in the sea, just you and me
Then on the beach we'll lay,
It may just seem like a far off dream
But maybe – one fine day!

*Kelvin Smith*

# AM I A NUTTER?

I'm on yellow tablets
And a daily red pill,
Friends say I'm mental
The doctor says I'm ill.

Two pink lunchtime
Two blue late at night,
Wop 'em down my cake hole
Flying like a kite.

What are they for?
Well I'm not really sure,
What have I got?
Is there a cure?

I stopped taking them months ago
There's no difference I can see,
Must be mind over matter
Shoving smarties inside me.

Am I really a nutter?
Who's qualified to say?
Compared to hundreds of others I meet
On National Nuttters' Day.

They see fairies in the garden
They see monsters in the bay,
Receive messages from the other side
So I think that I'm ok –
(*or at least in good company*)

*My Sister and Me*

# I KNOW THAT FACE

I can see it in your face
The pain that you spurt,
I can feel your depression
The wound and the hurt.

I can see that you're loveless
You've no place to hide,
Left in the wilderness
You're dying inside.

I know that face well
I've seen it before,
When I caught my reflection
As I walked out your door.

*Kelvin Smith*

# A SPERM'S DESTINY

I'm just an ordinary swimming sperm
Out to reach the eggs,
Hoping one day I can walk about
With body, arms and legs.

There are millions of us you know
And we all pray it could be me,
So for millions of us every Saturday night
It's just a lottery.

That's all I've ever thought of
It was my destiny,
To become a little girl or boy
With a mother to cuddle me.

I've been hanging around all my sperm life
My turn has come today,
As I'm thrust out from my man
As we both go all the way.

But it seems my days are numbered
I didn't get very far,
I'm just a stain on a satin dress
On the back seat of a car.

# MORE CONTENT

I never saw life's beauty
When I was just a lad,
The things I took for granted
Now all make me glad.

Just a walk down a country lane
On a sunny summer's day,
Once upon a time I run for fun
Now I smell the sweet bouquet.

And the hills I climbed yesteryear
And the years that I spent,
Not looking, hearing or smelling life
Now make me more content.

*Kelvin Smith*

# MUM SENT ME TO .......

Mum sent me to the butchers
And that was where I saw,
A Pig's head in a cardboard box
Just inside the door.

I'm sure I saw the box move
I thought, what shall I do?
What if he attacks me –
Will I get swine flu?

I ran home to mum so fast
With no sausages for brunch,
She shouted out, "What's the matter?"
I replied "They've gone for lunch".

Mum then sent me to the fishmongers
And that was where I saw,
A ginormous fish with ginormous teeth
Inside his ginormous jaw!

He made me catch my breath so quick
His big eyes spying me,
I thought our roles would reverse
And he'd have me for tea.

I ran all the way home to mum again
Where I heard her tutt,
"Where's the fish for our tea?"
I said the shop was shut.

*My Sister and Me*

## *Mum sent me to .......*

Mum looked at me so sternly
And that was when I saw,
A face more scarier than the fish
Or the pig's head by the door!

"Off to bed with your lies," she said
I tried to explain to Mum,
But the big fish chased me up the stairs
And the pig – it snorted some.

I came back down after a while
Mum wouldn't hear iffs or but,
'Cause when I said, "I'm hungry Mum,"
She said, "The Kitchen's Shut!"

*Kelvin Smith*

# THERE'S UNIQUE ....
# THEY CALLED ME GOLDIE!

Round and around
Around one more time,
Can you even see me?
Through the dirt and slime.

You watched me for a few days
Then the novelty wore off,
You've even stopped cleaning me out
Gasping deep in froth.

I'm just another goldfish
Doing what goldfish do,
I'll probably die in a few days
Then they'll flush me down the loo.

*My Sister and Me*

# HOW DO THE AUSTRALIANS? .....
## *(Tell Me Liz!)*

How do the Australians –
Walk around – outward bound – along the ground
Into town without a frown –
Upside down! – How?

Do they have suckers –
On their shoes – what's the news – perhaps use glues,
Do they have suckers on their shoes! –
Give us clues – what?

Why don't they fall off –
Into the sky – wave goodbye as the Aussies fly.
Why don't they fall into the sky
From where they lie – why?

Seems the Australians –
Would only say – that's our way, upside down we'll stay,
Seems the Australians would only say –
That's our way – so G'day – Wow!

*Kelvin Smith*

# SNORE – SNORE!

Snore – Snore!
Loud for sure
Every night from dad,
Snore – Snore!
Can't take no more
He's driving us all mad.

Snore – Snore!
What a bore
It's pointless when I nag him,
Snore – Snore!
Now it's war
Think I'll go and gag him.

Snore – Snore!
Snore some more!
I cannot get to sleep,
Snore – Snore!
I bang on his door
Then back to bed I creep.

Snore – Snore!
Now it's half past four
He just won't stop snoring,
Snore – Snore!
There must be a law
Non stop through till morning.

Snore – Snore!
I've padded my door
And hiding under the covers,
'Cause Snore – Snore!
Mum's started to snore
And so have both my bruvers!

# SHE CRIES

She cries in a whisper
She screams with no voice,
She cowers in the corner
'Cause she has no choice.

She suffers in silence
She breathes every word,
Of all her emotions
That only God's heard.

She smiles with no laughter
Her trust has long gone,
Her heart is so empty
Her life is so wrong.

*Kelvin Smith*

# STICK A PIN

I'm in a queue
What can I do?
There's nowhere I can hide,
They stick a pin
Into my skin
And draw the blood inside.

They check my eyes
Undo my flies
Then told to cough twice,
They've shaved off my hair
So how do they fair
Checking me for lice?

They inspect my mole
And every hole
And every blessed crack,
Then kitted out
Thin or stout
Same sized coloured black.

Made to sing
With the mandolin
Then drugged to make us sleep,
Tomorrow we'll wake
To spinach cake
And pushed around like sheep.

Then we'll queue
With the new
And at least one head will spin,
If there's a dud
The blood will flood
As they stick the pin in.

## CHOCOLATE BISCUITS

We'd all choose sunshine over the rain,
So why ignore chocolate biscuits and buy plain?

Come on, plain biscuits? Don't be a bore,
A nice cup of coffee and at least three or four.

I hate those people who nibble on the plain,
I can get a whole chocolate biscuit in again and again!

So please should you invite me round to tea,
Make sure there's chocolate biscuits with my coffee.

*Kelvin Smith*

# TEDDY ON THE SHELF

Teddy on the shelf
In the shop by himself
Waiting for someone to come,
To cuddle him tight
All through the night
And tickle his feet and his tum.

So I purchased sad Ted
Now he lives on my bed
Along with the other thirty three,
With the collection I've built
Piled high on my quilt
With no room left – sadly for me.

# PROMOTION SWAGGER!

Watch them walk different
When they get their promotion,
Their shoes actually get louder
With a military motion.

Hear them talk louder
They get more insecure,
They say it won't change them
As their dear friends get fewer.

Watch them forget
They once did the same,
Little mistakes that you're making
As they bollock and blame.

Notice accents changing?
Like they've taken a potion,
Funny how their hips sway
When they get their promotion.

Kelvin Smith

# WE WERE CHILDREN IN THE PLAYGROUND

We were children in the playground
These days they're not,
No time for fun and games
With the gadgets they got.

Tablets, computers and mobiles cost,
XBox – IPad – childhood lost.
Never had CD or a mountain bike,
Never heard of Reebok, Adidas – Nike.

We were children in the playground, 123,
Short grey trousers, graze your knee.
Sweeties in my pockets, lensies – shares,
Hopscotch in and out the squares.

No more racing in a sack,
Tag you're on it – got you back.
Queenie got the ball, who will win,
Run so fast and kick that tin.

Switch on your square box
Fresh air's gone,
Do you know your tables?
Wos happening – better log on.

# My Sister and Me

Ring a ring a Rosy, round and round,
British bulldog – get him down.
Snakes and ladders, join the dots,
Dolls in the cradle, prams and cots.

Computer fighting, couch potato – sleep,
Was piggy back fighting, land in a heap.
Affectionate bonny children was ABC,
Not it's arrogant and boring computerized We.

Enjoy your computers kids and your mobile phones,
Your pierced belly buttons and your pop ring tones.
Just got used to videos never mind DVDs,
And just bought a leather case for my LPs!

*Kelvin Smith*

# BETHLEHEM BY DAWN

Let's all go to Bethlehem
There's been a new King born,
If we leave right away
We'll be there by dawn.

I've heard his name is Jesus
With a heart that's full of love,
Sent by God Almighty
His son from up above.

If we follow the brightest star
We'll find baby Jesus there,
Patiently waiting to bless us all
With loads of love to share.

I cannot wait to see him
Amongst Angels full of grace,
I wonder if I'll get close enough
To see my Saviour's face.

So let's rejoice this holy night
For the new King born,
Sweet Jesus I came unto thee
Bethlehem by dawn.

# I USED TO BUT NO MORE

Take a pill, write my will
Now the house is sold,
Chance I might die tonight
Feeling oh so cold.

Sitting still – snow on the sill
The fire needs more coal,
Just sit and stare at the cupboard bare
And empty cereal bowl.

I used to laugh – no can't take a bath
No more soaking for a while,
Can't comb my hair or climb the stair
No more rinse and style.

I used to bleed – used to need
I used to love and kiss,
My life was chance, I used to dance
The simple things I miss.

I used to cry – now I die
No good being sore,
Running thoughts – vest and shorts
I used to but no more.

Life is hell – I'm just a shell
Part of me has gone,
And soon I'll be, I hope with thee
Hope heaven's not a con.

I'll soon be leaving because of my believing
I now know what's in store,
No aches or pain – no hurt again
I used to but no more.

*Kelvin Smith*

# THE GOONEY BIRD

THE ALBATROSS IS AT A LOSS
He's very upset I've heard,
Who's to blame for changing his name?
He's now the Gooney bird.

THE ALBATROSS IS VERY CROSS
The blackfooted type is stirred,
He often ponders while he wanders
Why he's called the Gooney bird.

In southern seas it's all a tease
Every day's a battle,
Don't be cross, wandering Albatross
It's only Tittle Tattle.

*My Sister and Me*

# IN LOVING MEMORY OF VASELINE

Thank heavens for Vaseline
It was always spread on me,
On my thumb and on my bum
And when I grazed by knee.

When I jammed my fingers
Mum greased the tips,
Also when I banged my head
And when I had chapped lips.

Gran put it on her patent shoes
How it made them shine,
Even on the rusty pulley
Of her washing line.

Dad always used it too
In the mirror he would stare,
He'd reach for the tin with Vaseline in
And rub it in his hair.

When my sister had a fight
And her bloody nose was leaking,
Mum rubbed the same Vaseline into her
That stopped her bed from squeaking.

Runner's nipple, stiff nuts and bolts
Footballers – Boxing Champ,
All the forces use it too
When they're confined to camp!

Suppose you could say that Vaseline
Was a must in every way,
And mum still keeps a tin of it
By the side of her bed today!

*Kelvin Smith*

# FISH FINGERS

Do fish really have fingers?
And if they do I suppose,
Supermarkets also sell packets
Of frozen fish toes.

Fish toes and chips please!
That doesn't seem right,
If you were given a fish toe –
Would you take a bite?

I really like fish fingers
But I won't eat fish toes,
Come to think of it – fish fingers?
Have they been up fish nose?

# BEST SAY GOODBYE

You don't love me
So why say you do?
Why make promises –
When you know they're not true?

Why say you're staying?
When we both know you'll go,
Why are you so high?
When you know that I'm low.

I've known that it's over
For a while I suppose,
These days when you kiss me
Your eyes never close.

I have to be realistic
Our life is a lie,
And although I still love you
Best say goodbye.

*Kelvin Smith*

# FACES

Faces in the bedroom, faces on the wall,
Faces on the stairway, impressions in the hall.

A presence in the bathroom, splashing in the bath,
Burning in the red coals, smoking in the hearth.

Faces in the darkness, whilst lying in your bed,
Floating in your memories, crowding in your head.

Creased up in your clothing, shining in your shoes,
Reflecting in the mirror, confronted in your booze.

Faces in the garden, appearing late at night,
Flying in the clouds above, appearing at first light.

Driving up the highway, staring in the street,
Faces that are genuine and faces that just cheat.

Faces you fall in love with, faces you despise,
Faces that are foolish and faces that are wise.

Faces that are familiar, faces fill your mind,
Faces that you've lost and faces that you'll find.

*My Sister and Me*

# I'VE BEEN A GLUTTON!

When my tummy's bulging
Because I've been a glutton,
I just wish that I could –
Undo my belly button.

*Kelvin Smith*

# ICE BLUE JEANS AND RECORDS

Taken for granted castle
Pass it every day,
The tower leaning towards us
Where we used to play.

Indoor market once buzzing
Especially Saturday,
Ice blue jeans and records
Made our bodies sway.

Frothy coffee in Pino's caff
Thought I'd be a star,
Writing silly lyric rhymes
Thought that we'd go far.

Sunless shades on a rainy day
Cool on Castle Street,
Ice blue jeans and polo neck
Threadbare shoes on feet.

Hanging around street corners
That was the thing to do,
Showing off my new record
Not second hand but new!

When I get home I'll dance again
I'm in heaven all day through,
'Cause my new record's on full blast
And my jeans are ice blue.

# LILLY MAY

Lilly May went walking
Sometime yesterday,
She has gone searching
For her heart that's gone astray.

Over hills and meadows
She picked a wild bouquet,
Until her blue summer sky
Suddenly turned grey.

Lilly found her true love
No more shall he stray,
Beneath the wild bouquet he lies
Next to Lilly May.

*Kelvin Smith*

# PAGE FROM A BOOK

You can rip a page from a book
But you can't rip a love from your heart,
A little will stay deep inside
Long after you've drifted apart.

You can rip a page from a book
But you can't rip a face from your mind,
Once you flick through your memory pages
You'll soon see the face that you find.

You can rip a page from a book
You can disregard something you've read,
But you'll always remember that song
Like a record it plays in your head.

You can rip a page from a book
But you can't rip the thoughts of that day,
That you shared with someone so special
'Cause forever with you it will stay …

You can rip a page from a book
But you'll take away the glory,
Because you'll end up with one page less –
And you won't know the story.

*My Sister and Me*

# OBSESSED WITH STARS

What's beyond the nightly stars?
Will we ever see?
If there's life up on Mars
Or anywhere in the galaxy.

Who's qualified to say
What's out there in the stars?
Mars, Galaxy – Milky Way
It's all just chocolate bars.

Kelvin Smith

# SCREAM (*Edvard Munch*)

Why can't they picture what I can see?
Is it because of my insanity?

Thoughts and fears are as clear as mud,
As the sun leaves the sky of rich red blood.

I can't separate reality from the dream,
Or the nightmare from nature's scream.

Colours on canvas mimics my face,
Photographing my fears in time and space.

The sun sets displacing the haunting sight,
There's a lucid resemblance of starry night.

Why can't they picture what I see?
'Cause they've yet to discover their own insanity.

*My Sister and Me*

# WAS

Come into my little world
Or I'll come into yours,
We can have what is now
And not what was – was.

Because was is over
Don't want was anymore,
I want to catch hold of was
And throw was out the door.

Come to think of it though
Was wasn't that bad,
And I think was probably was
The best was I ever had!

*Kelvin Smith*

# LITTLE BUDGIE

Here's my story of my former cage,
Where I was once – all the rage!

I had a little mirror and a ringing bell,
It used to be a nice place, where I used to dwell.

But then those days ended, no more life of joy,
No more let out of my cage and no more pretty boy!

My mirror gained a crack, with no peel in my bell,
They stopped cleaning me out – A budgie shouldn't smell.

I tried to be happy and chirped away,
But then someone banged my cage and made it sway.

My door flew open as my cage hit the floor,
It was my lucky break from my daily war!

I flew into a neighbour's house, she put me in a cage,
With a pretty budgie girl and I am all the rage.

Clean water every morning, let loose every afternoon,
I'm always called a pretty boy and my chirping's back in tune.

What more could a budgie want? With a mirror and a bell,
And a girlfriend to spend happy days – with a lovely budgie smell!

# MY WILLIE

My willie is a bugger
He's always in and out,
And if he doesn't get his way
He'll shrivel up and pout.

He'll rise up when excited
Then pounce just like a leopard,
All the women love him –
Willie – My German Shepherd.

Kelvin Smith

# NO MORE MUMMY

Where has Mummy gone?
Will she be back?
Feeling like a shop soiled teddy
Left on the rack.

The apron's gone I used to pull
My heart is empty, my eyes are full,
No more needles and no more wool
No more jokes and pranks to pull.

No more ruffling of my hair
No more carried up the stair,
No more sweeties now to share
I sit alone on Mummy's chair.

I used to leave my bed at night
If I dreamt and had a fright,
And into Mummy's bed – her clutch so tight
So I was safe and night-time bright.

Now the night is dark and I cannot sleep
No-one to run to, I dare not peep,
But the night is long and I soon fall deep
Crying for Mummy wears me to sleep.

Now I'm older, I still don't understand
Is Heaven fictitious or another land?
All I know is, I'm not alone as I stand,
I walk with my memories and my Mum holds my hand.

*My Sister and Me*

# SUSAN SWOT

There's a girl in my class
Her name is Sue,
She fancies me
And I like her too.

Because she's good at English
She's sick at maths,
And I can tell by her smell
That she takes regular baths!

When we do our homework
She always lets me look,
Deep inside her satchel
And her science book!

She's just like a dictionary
She knows everything,
Now she's promised to do my homework –
But here's the sting.

She said we'd have to kiss
In front of the class,
And I agreed to let her –
She can kiss my Ass!

*Kelvin Smith*

# WELL DRESSED MAN

What shall I wear tonight?
That's too silky - that's too bright.

That's too frilly - that is too,
That's too fine and that's see through.

That's too long – this is too short,
This is too itchy, that's too taught.

And as for these – I'm not wearing furs,
I'll look in my own wardrobe, I shouldn't be in hers!

*My Sister and Me*

# SILLY NAMES

Let's all catch the Barry train,
To the beach and home again.
And if it rains
Silly names – choo choo!

Let's all run down to the sand,
Take a paddle – hold dad's hand.
And if it rains
Silly names – Donkey!

Playing games – silly names
When it's not so sunny,
Who will win and make us grin
Shouting names so funny?

Let's dig a hole with my spade,
And show my Mum what I made.
And if it rains
Silly names – Bucket!

Then at the end of our special day,
On our trip home we will play.
And if it rains
Silly names – wee wee!

*Kelvin Smith*

# A VISIT TO ST. MARTINS

When the bells ring at St. Martins
Where the trees shade from the sun,
I'll stay with you a little while
Until my crying's done.

I'll talk to you in spirit
Just like I've done before,
I can see your faces so clearly
Through my eyes so sore.

Together now both as one
As a robin flutters down,
Is that you that's come to visit?
It takes away my frown.

Then when the bells stop ringing
And the sun deserts the sky,
I'll love and leave you one more time
Till I return again to cry.

# SILENCE NOT GOLDEN

I once said to my wife Gwen,
Don't ever speak to me again.

She smiled at me putting on her hat,
And said, "no problem, I can live with that".

Stuck for words, I called her a chancer,
And for obvious reasons –She didn't answer.

*Kelvin Smith*

# JINGLE BLOODY BELLS

Jingle Bells – Christmas sells
So much pressure for one day,
The kids want more than they've had before
Can't do it on my pay.

Jingle Bells – St Nicholas smells
Just wish that I could say –
No more toys for girls and boys
'Cause Santa's passed away.

*My Sister and Me*

# I DID BRING YOUR FLOWERS

I did bring you flowers
You never knew I came,
I saw another bouquet
With someone else's name.

I saw the kisses on the card
That he sent to you,
And that he'll love you always
(till there's someone new).

He sent you flowers
With kisses that'll roam,
I brought you flowers
And took my kisses back home.

*Kelvin Smith*

# THE GREAT CHEESE SHORTAGE

It's not a lie, it's not a tease,
I'm off to the moon to get more cheese.

I've got my bucket, I've got my spade,
I've got four sandwiches my mother made.

I can't fly there until tonight,
'Cause during the day it's out of sight.

Dad reckons it'll be all gone by June,
'Cause everyone's taking a chunk from the moon.

I think dad's right, it'll disappear soon,
'Cause when I looked last night – there was only a half moon.

*My Sister and Me*

# WITHOUT LOVE

Like a street that has no people
Like a church without a steeple
Without love nothing's right,
Like a child without its mother
Or a sister losing her brother
Having no-one to kiss goodnight.

Like a forest without its trees
Or a hive of deserted bees
Without love how would be feel?
Like a cub that's lost its way
Like a night without a day
Without love life is unreal.

Like a bell without it's peel
Or a cart with missing wheel
We all need love so much,
Like a world that cannot turn
Like a flame without a burn
We all need that loving touch.

Like a blue sky without its sun
Like a child deprived of fun
Love's a gift we all need,
Like a bride that's lost her ring
Or a bird with broken wing
From love life plants its seed.

And life to me is being free
And seeing the wonders of all earth and above,
My family and friends – the regards someone sends
But most of all being in love.

*Kelvin Smith*

# BLAA BLAA BALD SHEEP

BLAA BLAA Bald Sheep what happened to you?
Well Sir, honest sir, I haven't got a clue.

I woke up this morning, naked – what a pain,
Then saw my woolly jumper on, the little boy down the lane.

BLAA BLAA Bald Sheep, quiet as a mouse,
Yes Sir, Yes Sir, I sneaked into his house.

I stole back my jumper, ran the meadow in the rain,
Chased by the master and the little boy down the lane.

## LOVE ME ALWAYS

Mountains roll, oceans too,
And so does life, like me and you.

Mountains last, oceans too,
Yet life will die, like me and you.

So walk those mountains, sail oceans too,
And love me always, like I love you.

*Kelvin Smith*

# UNCLE FRED'S JUMPER

Nan decided to knit a jumper
For my Uncle Fred,
She forgot to leave a hole though
Through which he could put his head.

And so as not to upset her
He told her it was ace,
So from that day to this –
We've never seen his face.

He walked around unable to see
But he never made a fuss,
It had to happen I suppose
He got knocked down by a bus.

His last words through his woolly neck
Was "I don't like to moan,
But I think it would be appropriate
If I didn't have a head stone".

P.S It wasn't Uncle Bill's bus!

# STROLLING ON A MOON

Strolling on a moon
Whistling a tune
Wondering what tune it is,
Yet I whistled away
For the rest of the day
My life no longer a whizz.

I shiver and stir
'Cause it's cold up here
Wondering if I'll ever return,
Hungry for food
Enhances bad mood
And the oxygen I badly yearn.

How long must I wait?
I'll die at this rate
Let's hope hometime's soon,
It's getting so cold
And I'm getting old
Trying to remember that tune.

Asleep on this moon
December or June
It all just seems the same,
I'd like to refuse
But it's not mine to choose
And now I've forgotten my name.

*Kelvin Smith*

# I'M JUST A SNAIL

I'm just a snail, a snail in a shell,
Cramped up inside from where I dwell.

If I go for a walk, wherever it may be,
I have to carry my house and take it with me!

You'll never see me running, you'll never see me dance,
And should I go on holiday, it'll never be to France!

I'm always hiding in my shell from all,
'Cause when you're a snail – everything's tall.

Watch out for the birds, watch out for the car,
Those stupid chef blokes and newly laid tar.

Yes I'm just a snail – a snail in a shell,
Sometimes it's ok and sometimes it's hell.

And should I get lucky with a lady snail's rump,
I have to lift the whole house up, just for a hump.

But like the song says – should I ever roam,
Wherever I lay my shell, that's my home.

# SOMETIMES

Sometimes hanging on to a world record
Is harder than breaking it,
Sometimes eating someone else's cooking
Is harder than making it.

Sometimes it's harder being in love
Than actually faking it,
Sometimes it's harder accepting something
Than actually taking it.

Sometimes we screw up in life
Sometimes we blow it,
But we all do the same folks –
So crack on, don't throw it.

*Kelvin Smith*

# IF I COULD FLY

If I could fly – I'd fly
But not too high
I don't like heights,
And if I went too high
(If I could fly)
I'd probably have the shites.

And to have the shites on winter nights
At those great heights
Wouldn't be too grand,
So forgive the sights
If you see me in tights
When I come in to land.

*My Sister and Me*

# TURTLE SOUP

Take a photo – what a coup!
There's a turtle in my soup.

What's he doing on my plate?
It's a turtle – swimming mate!

What does it taste like? – Haven't a clue,
And I don't think I'm liable to.

'Cause I'll never eat turtle soup,
'Cause where there's turtle – There's turtle poop!

Kelvin Smith

# JUST THINKING

Thinking of yesterday compared to here and now
No-one seems the same,
Thinking of tomorrow – what can I do?
Who the hell's to blame.

Yesterday was my father
And now his life is done,
My turn to take the mantle
To be the father, not the son.

I can feel the tears
Burning in my eyes,
I wonder how long will it take
To reach my father's skies?

Everything's disappearing
Especially love and affection,
Folk don't seem so willing
Life's become rejection.

Children so helpless
Once true and kind,
Can turn so cruel
When they all unwind.

Watched as they grow
From day to day older,
Some become warmer people
While others become colder.

Copy as he walks
Copy as she talks
Sometimes it's a pity,
Some can stop it - while others cop it
And lose their identity.

## *Just Thinking*

The young girl has a doll,
Which is smacked when it's bad,
Doing as she see the world
Can sometimes be sad.

The young lad has a gun
And will imaginary kill,
And as seen on television –
The blood will spill.

Just thinking of today
Why's the world so grey?
Thinking perhaps of escape
Perhaps another way.

Today's another birth
Today's another killing,
Tomorrow's another refusal
Tomorrow's another willing.

Thinking of yesterday, looking at today
Nothing seems the same,
Thinking of yesterday, now looking at today
Unfortunately we're all to blame.

*Kelvin Smith*

# RAINING ANIMALS

"It's raining animals", my father said,
As I jumped quickly out of bed.

And to the window I looked through,
As my suspicions grew and grew.

And honestly! Guess what I saw?
'Twas raining cats and dogs galore!

*My Sister and Me*

# FEELNG GOOD

Having the sun shine on my face
Walking in falling snow,
Getting a call from a special friend
When I'm feeling low.

To hear a baby laugh
Getting space to be alone,
Just some time to find myself
No-one there to moan.

Seeing my children happy
They can make your heart burst,
Keeping calm and patient
When in the past I've cursed.

A cuddle from a loved one
When I am feeling blue,
Simple things make me feel good
Like holding hands with you.

Not to need and not to want
Content – a state of grace,
A gentle walk through the hills with you
With the sun upon my face.

*Kelvin Smith*

# DUMMY?

I asked my Mummy "Where's my dummy?"
Do you know what she said?
"If you want your dummy, my little chummy,
Then your father's asleep in bed."

*My Sister and Me*

# LETTER FROM HELL

This morning I received a letter, a letter from hell,
I ignored the letter and then my mind fell.

I couldn't reply – I had no address,
What could I do? I'm in a hell of a mess.

What is hell? It's not for the pure,
Well I'm not going there, that's for sure!

And as for you, Mr Devil esquire,
You're not taking me to the death of fire.

This morning I awoke, I awoke in hell,
I was awakened by the noise of the death ringing bell.

The fires were burning, yet the devil was dead,
I felt horns protruding out of my head.

I realised I'd been sent to take his place,
My turn to taunt the human race.

This morning I sent a letter – sent it from hell,
And this afternoon I died and another mind fell.

*Kelvin Smith*

# POOR SPIDER

As I saw a spider passing by,
It made me think and wonder why.

People kill such helpless things,
Not realising the grief it brings.

Then all of a sudden to devilish wit,
I picked up my foot and trod on it.
(I didn't really!)

*My Sister and Me*

# ORANGES ARE ORANGE

Oranges are orange, limes are lime,
Lemons are lemon – that makes a rhyme!

Apricots are apricot, peaches are peach,
Apples in our shop, are twenty pence each.

Red is for danger – green is for go,
Blue in the sky and the oceans below.

Bananas are yellow, picked when they're green,
When they're black, they're old – and so is the Queen.

Florins are silver, like the Lone Ranger's Horse,
On black and white telly, which is now colour of course.

Folk that are red heads, often have grit,
And I really love dunking a ginger biscuit.

Fruit on the top shelf, (an apple and peach)
I cannot eat them, 'cause I cannot reach.

I love the colours that shine everywhere,
Except the flipping colour of my flipping hair.

Oranges are oranges, limes are lime,
One day I will reach them, it just takes time.

*Kelvin Smith*

# SIT!

My father named our new dog Sit
Which I suppose was rather dumb,
Because everytime I call him now
He will never come!

*My Sister and Me*

# A WALK 'ROUND THE OLD RASPBERRY PASS

I went with a girl, the daughter of an earl
For a walk 'round the old Raspberry Pass,
I kissed her slow and she wanted to know
Why I'd taken her through the long green grass.

She was neat, her smell was sweet
And her velvet went with the weather,
I was rough and had no smelly stuff
And my coat was imitation leather.

We sat by a stream and I started to dream
And my hand naturally started to wander,
She hit me with speed, my nose began to bleed
She said I was faster than her brother's Honda.

I thought that's enough. I'm going to get tough
Even though she is an Earl's daughter,
So I told her to brace and with a smile on her face
She stood up and pushed me in the water.

I've usually been lucky – never been called ducky
Before by any young lass,
But it happened that day, when I went that way
For a walk 'round the old Raspberry Pass.

*Kelvin Smith*

# BOYS? – YUK!

Wedding bells, bridegroom smells
Walking down the aisle,
Wedding gown – what a frown
Mum says run a mile.

Far too young to catch bouquet flung
That's what Daddy said,
Dads and Mams – babies and prams
Play with dolls instead.

A bridesmaid dress – is no less
I'm told to give a twirl,
It'll always be, no boys for me
'Cause I'm Daddies little girl.

*My Sister and Me*

# YOU'RE GOING NOW

You're going now
You make my heart stall,
Both standing there unsure what to say
Freezing in the hall.

You open the front door
As the cold night blasts through,
You turn and smile at me –
I just don't know what to do.

The door slams behind you
Your frosted reflection gets smaller,
I just stand numb for a minute
Thinking perhaps I should call her.

But we've been over it a million times
It's something you have to do,
And it's something I have to endure
And that's being without you.

I sit by the fire devastated
The house already feels cold,
I feel so helpless – so dejected
So tired, so sick – so old.

It's a long night – I cannot sleep
My eyes burn with the lights,
Roll on daytime and tomorrow
I wished the wife never worked nights.

*Kelvin Smith*

# PARENTS LIE

""Eat your crusts," my Father said.
"It'll put curls upon your head".

So I ate more crusts than you've ever seen,
Then my hair fell out when I was seventeen!

# MR JANUARY COLD

As soon as January comes to freeze,
It won't be long before I sneeze.

Soon my hanky I'll unfold,
To deal with Mr January cold.

My nose will leak like a water pipe,
Non stop running as I wipe and wipe.

Hot water bottles and pillows piled high on my bed,
Trying to rid the cold in my head.

Why can't I be a friend and not a foe,
Of Mr January Cold that haunts me so?

I'm drained, I'm tired and feel so frail,
My brow so hot and my face so pale.

Oh Mr January Cold please hear my cry,
Why can't you for once pass me by.

Pass me by, I shan't miss you Sir,
'Cause I know you'll be back – January next year!

*Kelvin Smith*

# THE DODO

The Dodo is a no-no
And no more in Mauritius,
Unable to fly – then extinct but why?
It all seems so suspicious.

*My Sister and Me*

# BLUE HILL (*Bryn Glas*)

When I get to Blue Hill
I will meet with you,
We'll tell each other stories
Like we used to do.

We'll lie next to each other
Amongst the lush of blue,
I'll tell you that I've missed you
You'll say you missed me too.

We'll hold each other tightly
Whether right or wrong,
Cherishing our time together
'Cause Blue Hill don't last long.

The Hill will soon turn green again
It means I cannot stay,
And like our love until next year
Blue Hill fades away.

*Kelvin Smith*

# FOUR LEAF CLOVER

I've been searching for a four leaf clover,
I've been to Edinburgh and to Dover.

I have searched my whole life through,
Checked Wales out – Ireland too!

But no matter wherever I've been bound,
That four leaf clover can't be found.

And if I'm honest, I've never been to Dover,
It was just a place that rhymed with Clover!

*My Sister and Me*

# DAD

Dad! Where are you Dad?
Can you hear me call your name?
Let me see you for just a minute Dad
Do you still look just the same?

Oh come on Dad – just a quick cuddle
And then I'll let you be,
Just a wave or whistle a song
Come back and visit me.

Dad! Where are you dad?
Are you on that shining star?
Are you really up in Heaven Dad?
Please tell me where you are.

I sometimes smell your aftershave
When I picture you I'm glad,
Before the time Jesus took you –
You spent with me as Dad.

Dad, since you left Mum's been ill
And I've been very sad,
Please visit me in my dreams
I love and miss you Dad.

*Kelvin Smith*

# BRITISH TOILET WEATHER

The British weather's like a toilet
It flows just like a tap,
It always seems to be peeing down
The weather's always crap.

# LONDON MARATHON
## (Debbie's Wish)

I'm running the London in April
I've read all about the wall,
I've bought new knickers and a vest
Cheap at the market stall.

I've tried various types of training
But I'm never in the mood,
I can't get on with hill runs
And the fartlek seems so rude.

I'm up to two a day now
Soon be three then four,
Got to be honest that's mars bars though
Got to get out that door.

It always seems so bloody cold
These winter mornings so dark,
And I'm always knackered anyway
Just half way round the park.

I ran the London in April
I hate that market stall,
My knickers snapped at 2 miles
And at '3' I hit that wall!

# GOD IS .......

### *Lyrics for brighter light music – Toronto.*
### *Music written by Mary Ellen Pierce*

God is the rain
God is the sun,
God is the love
Inside everyone.

God is the sky
God is the earth,
God is the air
We breathe from our birth.

God is the fruit
That bears the new seeds,
God is the answer
To all of our needs.

God is the water
That quenches our thirst,
God is the father
That puts us all first.

God is our life
Our laughs and our cries,
God is our sight
We see through our eyes.

God is our listener
That we can depend,
God is our beginning
And God is our end.

# DO YOU EVER?

### (*Lyrics written for Richard Butler Music*)

Do you ever feel happy?
Do you ever feel sad?
Do you ever think inside yourself –
You could be going mad?

Do you ever tend to worry?
Have you ever stopped to think?
Do you ever shake it off –
Smiling with a wink?

Have you ever really fallen?
Have you ever really cried?
Have you ever told a story –
And all along you've lied?

Chorus
Well if you're really honest
And if you're really true,
You'll say yes I have
And sometimes yes I do.

Have you ever had a love?
Do you ever tend to hate?
Have you ever had a friend –
That you could call a mate?

Have you ever felt like laughing
After someone made you cry?
And have you ever been let down
And all you want to do is die?

Have you ever neglected yourself
To think of another?
Do you ever put yourself first
Long before any other?

Repeat Chorus

*Kelvin Smith*

# THE MIDDLE OF SOMEWHERE

In the middle of somewhere, far far away,
Is closer than you think if you leave yesterday.

You can't go tomorrow and you can't leave today,
And you'll have to walk backwards if you leave yesterday.

No-one's ever been there – well nearly everyone,
The moon only comes out, the same time as the sun.

There's just one rule – wear turtle socks,
That you'll find with clouds in an orange box.

Should you ever get there, be sure not to stay,
Unless you leave the week before you arrived there on that day.

Perhaps we'll go together, backwards we will stray,
To the middle of somewhere, if we leave there yesterday.

# DREAM YOU LIFE AWAY

We dream of death in life
So do we dream of life in death?
Perhaps dreaming immediately of life
As we take our last breath.

So am I dead now?
And my life is just a dream,
And everything I see
Is just a re-occurring theme.

A never ending dream
In a never ending death,
Giving a never ending life
When I take my last breath.

*Kelvin Smith*

# KANGAROOS IN KENT?

Albert John was fed up of the holes,
Appearing on his lawn from mischievous moles.

He devised a plan to dig a big hole,
To oust every persistent-hole digging mole.

He got his spade and dug and dug,
Hoping to catch the hole digging thug.

He dug night and day, he didn't stop,
The hole digging mole was for the chop.

The hole became a tunnel that run for miles,
With stacked up earth, in piles and piles.

But as the weeks went by, not a thing,
Then a final dig – one final sting.

The darkness of his tunnel suddenly turned bright,
Because there below him he found daylight.

His plan for the moles became a failure,
Especially when he realised he was in Australia!

He rushed back home and arrived at dawn,
To find kangaroos jumping on his lawn.

I know this catastrophe was never meant,
But that's why there's moles in Sydney and kangaroos in Kent!

*My Sister and Me*

# DOWN BY THE SEA

Down by the sea
Sipping iced tea
Watching the girls go by,
I was taken aback
When a girl smiled back
And thinking I caught her eye -

Decided to see
If she really liked me
And hoping my cheeks wouldn't red,
I decided to follow
By my aspirations were hallow
When a seagull shit down on my head.

Kelvin Smith

# PEARLY QUEENS

I dreamt last night, my heart took flight,
Thinking that you just might – (still love me).

We went up to London on the red choo-choo,
Like we used to do - (when you loved me).

Pearly Queens and Pearly Kings
All dressed up in pearly things,
Love was roses and birds that sing
Shopping with kisses for wedding rings.

Heads out the window, our hearts aglow,
Singing along with the radio – (when you loved me).

Chocolate ice-cream with sauce on top,
All washed down with raspberry pop – (when you loved me).

Pearly Queens and Pearly Kings
Funny what a new love brings,
Cries and sighs and gooey things
That turns to hate and nasty stings.

I dreamt today that you just walked away,
As I was going to say – (I still love you).

But if there's no flame, it's not the same,
There's no-one else for us to blame – (it's over).

Pearly Queens and Pearly Kings
All dressed up in pearly things,
Now the Pearly Queen has left her king
And flown away with the bird that sings.

I went up to London on the red choo-choo,
Like we used to do – (without you)

Pearly Queens …..

*My Sister and Me*

# BARBARELLA

I saw Barbarella
Outside the Beer Keller,
Cosy with a fellar
Under his umbrella.

Someone should tell her
To leave his umbrella,
'Cause I don't think he realises –
Barbarella's a fellar!

*Kelvin Smith*

# LOST KITTEN

The snow is falling and I am calling
I can't see through the storm,
I'll search for you all night through
To keep you safe and warm.

I think I see – you running to me
And then you disappear,
The snow gets deeper, the road steeper
I shed another tear.

At break of day, the storm at bay
I head off homeward bound,
To tell young folk, whose hearts are broke
That you have not been found.

I whispered a rare desperate prayer
Then fell deep in the snow,
To weak to rise, I closed my eyes
No further could I go.

With my hopes dashed, my life flashed
Exhausted by the chase,
I resigned to the thought my life was bought
Until you licked my face.

I felt your fur that was to spur
My eyes again to see,
I found strength to roam, those few miles home
Carrying you close to me.

*My Sister and Me*

# LOVERS' DAY

Dining by candlelight
With nothing to say,
Is crap when you're married
On Valentine's Day.

*Kelvin Smith*

# OBVIOUS

Without the night there'd be no dawn,
There's only death 'cause we were born.
We cannot stop unless we start,
We couldn't live without a heart.
And what the sun without a moon?
And music too without a tune.
We couldn't live without the rain,
Couldn't hurt but for the pain.
If there was no lending there'd be no debt,
If there was no armies there'd be no threat.
If there was no bullet there'd be no gun,
Without a laugh there'd be no fun.
Without animals there'd be no meat,
But we'd still get by there's loads to eat.
Unless there's four it's not a quad,
Pointless praying if there's no God.
You can't undo all you've done,
You cannot win until you've won.
You're only frightened when there is fear,
You cannot cry without a tear.
If you've never had – you'll never miss,
No affection – she shouldn't kiss.
No regulations unless there's rules,
No wise men unless there's fools.
There's no shallow unless there's deep,
No path is high unless it's steep.
There is no high unless there's low,
You can't forget what you don't know.
There is no quench without a thirst,
You haven't swore unless you've cursed.
And this too should make you cuss,
'Cause all I've wrote is obvious!

# NOT FLAT?

As soon as I found
That the world was round
I obviously realised that,
The answer I sought
Is not what I thought
'Cause I always thought it was flat.

I'm quite sound
With it being round
But then I don't really care,
At least when it's round
I won't fall off the ground
As opposed to it being oblong or square!

If it was flat
I couldn't do that
No matter where ever I'm bound,
So I just want to say
We should all shout Hooray!
For the fact that our great world is round.

*Kelvin Smith*

# ARE WE NEARLY THERE MAM?

"Are we nearly there Mam
How long will it be,
How many more miles – Mam
Mam – can you hear me?"

"How much longer now Mam?
I'm starving for my tea,
Are we nearly there, Mam?
I'm busting for a pee!"

"How much further now Mam
Before we see the sea?
Can we stop somewhere Mam?
I'm awfully thirsty".

"I can see the fairground
And look there's the sea!
What time are we going home Mam
How long will it be?"

*My Sister and Me*

# TOAST MY BIRTHDAY

I believed that I'd receive
Some goodies through the post,
What a shame – nothing came –
Had some tea and toast.

Thought a while, tried to smile
Nothing second post,
Tissues near – wiped a tear
Had some beans on toast.

End of the day – bed I lay
Not a day to boast,
No more sorrow – check tomorrow
Had some tea and toast

*Kelvin Smith*

# GAVIN THE PIG

Gavin the Pig doesn't live in a sty,
He lives in a flat by the river Wye.

He escaped from a farm just outside York,
He liked being Gavin – he didn't want to be pork.

He'd seen his picture on the side of a tin,
So he got out quick, so as not to be in.

It was a long way to walk to the River Wye,
'Cause as you all now – pigs don't fly!

*My Sister and Me*

# CWTCH (*Cuddle*)

It's time to cwtch
When the weather's cold,
Give kids a cwtch
When they're good as gold.

We all need a cwtch
When we've been hurt,
'Cause a cwtch does work
And that's a cert.

Just a loving cwtch
When you're not well,
Is better than medicine –
A magic spell.

Time to cwtch
When you say goodbye,
When you fall in love
Or when a friend may cry.

You're never to butch
To have a cwtch
No matter what the weather,
Cwtching's a blast
Make hearts beat fast
Cwtch-up cwtch-up forever!

*Kelvin Smith*

# PONTY PARK

Up like a lark to Ponty Park
When the sun is beaming,
They make you stare, the butes so rare
'Cause Ponty girls are dreaming.

Sunbathe all day, bikini clad lay
Everyone's a cocker,
Ponty's the place for a beauty to chase
You can stuff Tenerife and Minorca.

# ALONE AT NIGHT
## (A Non Rhymer Professor!)

When the light goes out
I am alone,
It's a long night
A long lonely night,
I hear every noise I wouldn't normally hear,
I stare into the blackness,
Is there someone there?
Is there someone behind me?
Is there someone watching me?
Are they ready to pounce?
Will they slit my throat?
Will they smother me?
Someone's here, who is it?
Leave me alone!
I can hear then breathing,
I can hear them getting nearer,
I can feel them by the bed,
I can see them –
Oh! It's the bloody dog!

*Kelvin Smith*

# WHAT'S THE CRACK GIRLS?

Dearest Ladies please listen to me
'Cause I know you're quite inclined,
To worry what us men think
About the size of your behind.

Well let me tell you ladies
And this is absolutely true,
Us men love all types of bums
We really really do!

So next time she asks you lads
Does my bum look big in this,?
Just get down on your knees
And give her butt a kiss.

*My Sister and Me*

# ACROSS THE SEA

On the phone across the sea,
Just a voice you and me.

You seem so close yet far away,
When you phone me every Saturday.

As we chat I imagine your face,
Sat next to me here both in one place.

Laughs, sighs and memories pour,
It's as if you're here, perhaps next door.

On the phone across the sea,
Just a voice you and me.

Bye for now, and by the way,
I'll see you again next Saturday.

*Kelvin Smith*

# (Aunty) QUEENIE GOT THE BALL

Throw a ball against the wall
To songs and made up rhymes,
Kick a ball against the wall
Probably a million times.

Told to go away with that ball today
Far away from her wall,
And if I don't – then she won't
Give me back my ball.

But I have got – one last shot
Against your wall today,
We then call – Queenie got the ball!
Then run away and play.

*My Sister and Me*

# A WEEKEND'S MURDER

Saturday morning
My day off boring
Another weekend of strife,
Done the polishing
Hung some washing
For a trying wife.

Sunday morning
Not so boring
The best since I've been wed,
Done no polishing
And hung no washing
'Cause I've hung the wife instead.

Kelvin Smith

# FALLEN CROSS

There's a fallen cross of a tragic loss
Where the ivy's overgrown,
Constant shuns as no-one comes
To the grave of the unknown.

People pass the uncut grass
Without a second glance,
Walk on by, no thoughts or sigh
It doesn't stand a chance.

Then so do I, walk on by
No-one gives a toss,
Who will save the unknown grave
Of the forgotten fallen cross.

# OOPS (*A Man's Forgetfulness*)

Why's that suitcase on top of the wardrobe?
I never put it there,
Why is there a brush on the dressing table?
I don't have any hair.

Why are there running shoes under the bed?
I don't run any more,
Why are there dresses in my wardrobe
And knickers in the drawer?

Why is there a lead hanging in the kitchen?
The dog died years ago,
Why is there a picture of a woman in the lounge?
I'm sure I don't know.

Why are the walls papered with roses?
When I painted them royal blue,
Why is there a number four on my front door
When I live at No 2?

- oops

Kelvin Smith

# IS HEAVEN IN THE SUN?

No matter what else they have done,
They'll never penetrate the blazing sun.

An invincible fortress day and night,
When we're at death we see the light.

Heavenly father and the son,
Do we mean sun – are they one?

We could never search, so we'll never find,
It's impossible, we'd burn and blind.

Who am I to think that I can suss,
But could sunbeams be a way of watching us?

And scientists do they really know,
Of a place in life they'll never go?

From the depths of the sea, to Mars or the Moon,
But inside the sun – that's a different tune.

There's nothing better than the sun on your face,
The warmth, the healing – amazing grace.

Is the sun continually watching earth,
Through our life to death to re-birth?

I may be right – I may be wrong,
We'll soon know for sure when we're gone.

And when the light does finally come,
Wonder if it'll be the Heavenly Sun.

*My Sister and Me*

# HYPOCHONDRIAC

I'm fed up of all my ills,
Always seem to be taking pills.

I got aches and pains
With pin pricked veins
And a swelling in my calf,
I feel sick
And my knees just click
And my bloody back's in half.

I wish I felt a bit more fit,
I always think perhaps this is it!

What's this lump?
What's this bump?
What's this on my head?
Can't feel my jaw
My throat is sore
And now my face is red!

The colour of my urine needs a test,
Now I got a pain in my chest!

The doctor's fed up
The wife says shut up
I know that it's a fact,
They moan at me
Because unfortunately
I'm a Hypochondriac.

There's one consolation – which is brill,
If I die, I can't be ill!

*Kelvin Smith*

# A FEW MORE NURSERY RHYMES REVISITED AS A KID

### GUTSY JACK HORNER

Gutsy Jack Horner – sicked in the corner
After scoffing so much pie,
But he still scoffed more then run out the door
'Cause he had diahorrea as well that's why.

### TEN IN THE BED

There were ten in the bed and the stupid one said –
"Light some dynamite – light some dynamite",
So they all lit some dynamite and blew themselves up –
There were ten in the bed, but now they're all dead,
Can't roll over – can't roll over …..

### HUMPTY DUMPTY

Humpty Dumpty sat on Paul,
Humpty Dumpty wore a dress to the ball.
All the king's horses and all the king's men,
Started visiting Humpty again and again!

### BOBBY SHAFTOE

Bobby Shaftoe sunk at sea
Lost a leg and his willy,
He's coming back to marry me?
I don't think so Bobby Shaftoe!

# SHORT LOVE
## (Written For Sister Hayley's Wedding)

They kissed under the romantic moon,
Love was now and marriage soon.

They looked each other in the eyes,
As thunder let rip from the blackening skies.

They ran for shelter to a nearby tree,
Her caring for him and he for she.

They held each other very tight,
They may have been wet, but they were happy that night.

They promised to love each other forever,
With unhappy times – they would be never.

And many more promises they'd soon make on oath,
Then lightning struck the tree and killed them both.

*Kelvin Smith*

# PEACEFUL WATERS

Peaceful waters gently flow,
Past the trees all stood in row.

Through the village, then the town,
Past the palace and the crown.

She'll cross the boundaries flowing free,
Then sets her sights to open sea.

To rise and fall once again,
To build the rivers from her rain.

Where peaceful waters gently flow,
Giving life to all we know.

# IN THE GENES

They always said Grandad was ugly
And I think it's such a sin,
They also said that I, the youngest sibling
Actually looked like him!

*Kelvin Smith*

# SCHOOL DINNER MONEY

Dinner money in my pocket
To make sure I'll be fed,
But I will spend it playtime
On sweets and pop instead.

If my Father finds out
He is bound to shout,
And I'll be running up them stairs
From another clout.

I don't get pocket money
Like the other kids every day,
So to buy nice goodies just like them
My dinner money pays my way.

So I'll go on buying sweets and pop
I can put up with the shout,
And starving until I get home
And the occasional stinging clout.

*My Sister and Me*

# PETE THE PEACOCK

A peacock by the name of Pete,
Couldn't find shoes to fit his feet.

So Pete flew off to foreign lands,
And walked about on feathered hands.

Then as he shopped in dear Toulouse,
He found a pair of peacock shoes.

So if you see a peacock in the street,
Wearing shoes – say hi to Pete!

*Kelvin Smith*

# TICK-TOCK

Tick–Tock, the seconds sound,
Watching the hands go round and round.

The seconds tick fast, the minutes turn slower,
Watching time pass hour after hour.

Day turns night – night turns day,
March turns April – hair turns grey.

The years creep up and soon unfold,
One day you're young – next you're old.

Years turn slow yet life goes fast,
Get yourself out and have a blast.

Grab those seconds – clasp the hours,
Dance till midnight – buy her flowers.

Roll in snow and fallen leaves,
Get stuck in – roll up your sleeves.

Tick-Tock, the seconds sound,
You're a long time lying underground.

# JOEY DRAKERS

Joey Drakers robbed the bakers
He had to steal some dough,
Being a nutter, he stole bread and butter
What a dopey Joe!

Gangland boss – Big Ted from Rhos
Didn't think it funny,
He explained to Joe, the slang name dough –
Told him it meant money.

So Joey Drakers robbed another bakers,
To pay off boss Big Ted,
What did he steal? Two loaves of wholemeal!
Poor Joey's now Brown Bread.

*Kelvin Smith*

# HAPPY FAMILIES?

Blood's thicker than water – well is it really?
What does that tell us – water flows freely.

We're born in love to family – families have to stick,
Sometimes for the sake of it – friendship seems to click.

We tend to choose a good friend – families we've no choice,
Families are pubic transport – a good friend's a Rolls Royce.

We all love our families – friends arrive through fate,
And when we have a problem, it's nice to see a mate.

Friends are attached by friendship, a good friend won't let go,
Families are attached by Sunday Lunch, friendship tends to grow.

We all know that it's a fact – when life tends to fall,
It won't be the family, it'll be a friend that tends to call.

# POOR MOUSE

"Please don't eat me", said the mouse to the cat,
The cat replied "Oh I wouldn't do that".

So the mouse jumped down off the gate post,
And the cat ate him up with a slice of toast.

*Kelvin Smith*

## YOU'LL SOON REALISE

Ever feel lonely with nothing to do?
Thinking there's no-one you can turn to.

Ever feel hard done by? It's always you,
That works the hardest and one of the few.

Then realise the lost and know you're found,
Imagine being deaf not hearing a sound.

Think of the blind that cannot see,
Those wrongly imprisoned that cannot be free.

Think of those that cannot talk,
The unfortunate that cannot walk.

The homeless that roam around wild,
Desperate parents that lose a child.

What about the aged left all alone,
Sitting unwanted chilled to the bone.

The starving families overseas,
Children with illnesses in all countries.

When you stop to think of the heartache and cries,
There's millions worse off, you'll soon realise.

# ANGEL

I saw an angel yesterday
While I sat and cried,
My tears stopped flowing when –
She sat down by my side.

I felt so warm and content
The hurt just flew away,
And then so did the angel
Thank God for her I pray.

*Kelvin Smith*

# SPOTTED DICK

My friend Dick was oh so sick
They sent him to the docs,
'Cause he had lots and lots of spots
That was diagnosed Chicken Pox.

The doc said "bed! With your hot head",
Then with all his strength he mustered,
Ironically – spotted dick for tea
All covered in loads of custard.

## MY QUESTIONS

Why are we here, here on this earth?
Why is there death when there is birth?

How many expressions make a face?
What will become of the human race?

When will it end, this world of ours?
Will it be finished by the great powers?

These are the questions I want to ask,
But for anyone to answer is to big a task.

Nobody really knows why or even how,
Nobody's ever really known and nobody knows now.

Who really made man and created this earth?
What's beyond the stars and what's it worth?

Is there a God and was there a resurrection?
Can someone honestly, truly, answer my question?

Because these are the questions I want to ask,
But for anyone to answer is too big a task.

Nobody really knows why or even how,
Nobody's ever really known and nobody knows now.

*Kelvin Smith*

# ALWAYS

When someone says always
They don't mean what they say,
Always aint tomorrow
Just something said today.

Always aint forever
'Cause always doesn't last,
Always aint the future
It's just said in the past.

# REFLECTION

I look into the mirror
What do I see?
Well I see someone –
And that someone's not me.

I know it's my reflection
But it's never been true,
Because I can see past it –
My reflection's see through.

I lift my left hand
And I get a fright,
My reflection doesn't copy
Surely that isn't right.

My reflection's no reflection
Of my former self,
Everyone says the same thing –
You've got your health!

Think I'll smash that mirror
Ye, that's what I'll do,
And stop that other person
Masking what's true.

Mirror Mirror on the wall,
No more hanging in the hall.
False reflections now refrain,
From turning other ghosts insane.

*Kelvin Smith*

# AUNTIE MINNIE

Auntie Minnie on all fours
Doing all her household chores,
I only wish when she scrubbed floors
Auntie Minnie wore some drawers!

*My Sister and Me*

# IF EVER I COME BACK

If ever I'm reborn again
It won't be as a cat or a dog,
A horse or even an elephant
I'll be a leaping humping frog.

I'll laze about on lily ponds
Till my mating song is sung,
Then pursue my early evening meal
Catching flies upon my tongue.

But the biggest thrill I'll enjoy
Is when mating frogs indulge,
Non stop you know for 28 days
No wonder their eyes bulge.

I can put up with a croaky voice
And living in a bog,
If I'm to be born once again
As a leaping humping frog!

*Kelvin Smith*

# BEGGAR?

Walking through the city
Passed a beggar in the street,
Noticed he was wearing better trainers
Than I had upon my feet.

He said that he was homeless
Listened to him moan,
As he felt his Levi pockets
For his ringing phone.

He lit a cigarette up
Then quickly gave a dab,
I walked on through the pouring rain
As he hailed a taxi cab.

# MY EPITAPH
# (Or One Of Them!)

When you die
Here you lie
Just happens it's my turn,
Just want to say
I chose this way
'Cause I didn't want to burn.

Please agree
Don't cry for me
As you read my epitaph,
Dry your eyes
Say your goodbyes
Just think of me and laugh.

Kelvin Smith

# JUST ANOTHER DAY

I awoke this morning, as you do,
Toasted some bread and made a brew.

Made a few sarnies – my box for lunch,
A lump of cheese and an apple to crunch.

Put on my coat and my Gilbert cap,
And it's off to work 'cause I'm a grafting chap.

Another long day – one last cup of tea,
Picked up my bag, my flask, my key.

Looked out the window and saw it rain,
Thought, oh sod it – went back to bed again.

*My Sister and Me*

# DIVORCE

I once asked my mum what divorce meant,
She broke it down instantly, this is how it went –

    D – is for Dickhead – your father's real sad,
    I – is for Irritating habits that drove her mad.
    V – Is for Vile – your father's just mad,
    O – is for Orgasm, I've never had.
    R – is for Randy (Dad was he reckons),
    C – is for Crap (about 20 seconds).
    E – Is for Eternity? I don't think so,
    Divorce is like Heaven – an all over glow.

It's amazing actually, they're both still together,
Dad calls Mum June and Mum's name is Heather!

*Kelvin Smith*

# THE LAST FEW DAYS OF A SPARROW

I am a little sparrow
I fly from tree to tree,
With some 2.2. slugs in my head
Some bastard shot in me.

I'm like a baby's rattle
I jingle as I fly,
Looks like it's just a few days
Before I'm going to die.

I never saw who it was that got me
My eyes closed as I got hit,
But just to be sure of some revenge
I fly over folk and shit.

## ABSENT FRIENDS

I often wonder where they all are now
Those good friends from the past,
We promised to see each other soon
But time has gone so fast.

Good friends today are hard to find
Not like the forgotten gang,
We laughed and joked and danced all night
'til the early morning we sang.

When I take a drink I stop and think
I see their faces before me,
I imagine they're here like once they were
Though I know they'll never again be.

An old birthday card can make me sad,
With the signature on the inside,
A twenty first key that was sent to me
And by a friend the ribbon was tied.

I remember the sight – I remember the night
To think of them now makes me smile,
There was never a row, where are they now?
Haven't seen them for quite a while.

To absent friends one and all
Sadly though you can't hear my call,
To all of whom I said goodbye
And often I wonder the reason why.

A toast to the future and what it sends
But most of all to absent friends,
Whatever you're doing, whatever your trends
I drink to you my long lost friends.

*Kelvin Smith*

# A '99' PLEASE

It should have been
At seventeen
Every living schoolboy's dream,
A girlfriend of mine
Asked for a sixty nine
And I went and bought her an ice cream.

*My Sister and Me*

# JACK AND BILL

Jack and Bill went up the hill
To look for Teddy's daughter,
Jack came down with a sorry frown
'Cause Bill was the one who caught her.

She and Bill both caught a chill
After doing things they weren't aughta,
Bill got a thump because of the lump
That's developed on Teddy's daughter.

Now poor old Bill is alive and well still
And living with Ted and his daughter,
He calls Ted – Dad, 'Cause the lump's now a lad
Oh if only Jack had caught her.

Kelvin Smith

# IF GRANDAD WOULD ONLY DIE
## (His Favourite Poem!)

There'd be no more fag ends in his tea,
No more wiping up his pee.
No more scum in the bath,
No more spitting in the hearth.
No more fetch and bring,
No more playing with his thing.
No more moan, cough or sigh,
If Grandad would only die.

No more getting in a state,
No more licking of his plate.
No more teeth in a glass,
No more wiping of his arse.
No more swearing when he falls,
No more flashing, bums and balls.
No more zipping up his fly,
If Grandad would only die.

No more disgusting smelly breath,
No more shouting 'cause he's deaf.
No more burping, farting – sicking,
No more finger up his nose and flicking.
No more strokes or cardiac arrest,
No more banging on his chest.
No more mess like a pig sty,
If Grandad would only die.

No more putting back to bed,
No more wondering, "is he dead"?
No more losing his bunch of keys,
No more scratching – has he got fleas?
No more wiping the ever flow,
Of his nose – he has to go!
Oh Grandad couldn't you try?
If Grandad would only die.

# MORE HONEST

I once wouldn't admit it –
But yes I pray,
That's because I'm more honest –
Than I was yesterday.

*Kelvin Smith*

# THE MOLE

There is a mole story I can tell,
Of a mole I know so well.

It doesn't move or make a sound,
Nor does it live down underground.

It never digs or makes a hill,
In fact this mole is always still.

It's over sixty years old now,
Which for a mole – you might think wow!

But there's a twist to all I've said,
It is the mole upon my head.

# WHERE ONCE THE GREEN GRASS LAY

The green hills are leaving now
Gradually they fade away,
Being replaced by red bricks
Where once the green grass lay.

The picnic spots are leaving too
Once where folk went lazing,
No more flowers, birds or bees
And no more cattle grazing.

Down come the trees, up go the buildings
An ever flowing money fountain,
The earth's turned over, foundations put in
As red bricks are pushed further up the mountain.

There's a housing estate I remember
It was a field when I was a child,
Where we used to play having so much fun
And where once the flowers grew wild.

What's going to happen when it's all gone?
Because it's fading every day,
I now look to where disasters took
What nature gave to us – away.

The green hills are leaving now
Gradually they fade away,
Being replaced by red bricks
Where once the green grass lay.

Kelvin Smith

# WHERE'S JESUS WHEN YOU NEED HIM?

Bills pile up on the passage floor
Don't open them for a while,
Look into the mirror as depression sinks in
My whole world seems so vile.

Lost my job, family split
Life's a downward slope,
Helpless, hurting and feeling useless
Accepting I can't cope.

But when they ask "How are you"?
I smile and say I'm fine,
There aren't many that actually care
These troubles aren't theirs but mine.

I feel so alone
I sit around and hide,
Hungry for food and for love
Have no-one to confide.

Where's Jesus when you need him?
I couldn't help but think,
Tears stain my thinning face
As my faith begins to shrink.

But eventually I came out the other side
Then wrote this little rhyme,
Where was Jesus when I needed him?
He was with me all the time.

# I FELL ....

I fell for the face
And not the girl,
So I loved the shell
And not the pearl.

And when you love the shell
And not the girl,
You'll never ever face
That precious pearl.

*Kelvin Smith*

# DON'T IT MAKE YOU LAUGH?

Apples rot on the British tree,
While tins of it arrive from Italy.

We send our sand out to Iran,
And buy Welsh dolls from plastic Japan.

Frozen cauliflowers arrive from across the sea,
As spaghetti leaves our shores for Italy!

Don't it make you laugh – don't it make you wonder?
This great farming country of ours gets its butter from down under.

Pets are cuddled while wildlife gets fewer,
People are dying from which there's a cure.

All countries say that they want peace,
But will war and terrorism ever cease?

Don't it make you laugh – don't It make your cry?
By the time you get your pension it's almost time to die.

The telly licence is up again in price,
Yet everything we're watching, we've all seen at least twice.

Millions are starving overseas -
While mousetraps are set with lumps of cheese.

Don't it make you bloody laugh – don't it make you sad?
They say the best times of our lives – are the ones we've already had.

# CEASE YOUR HURT

For your hurt to cease
Make your peace
Show you love not hate,
Say your goodbyes
And halt future cries
Before it's far too late.

*Kelvin Smith*

# OUR SUNNY SPECIAL DAY
## (With Callum, Aged Two)

If I could keep the sun up
And make this day last,
I'd never need to look back
And reminisce the past.

This day would last forever
Forever me and you,
Just running 'round together –
The sky forever blue.

You'd never ever leave me
Cuddles – giggles and play,
Our whole life playing in the sun
Would be our sunny special day.

When you put your arms around me
It's the best feeling I must say,
To feel your face next to mine
In our sunny special day.

The things you said made me laugh
From the minute that you came,
You run and jump into my arms
Love hear you call my name.

So if I could keep the sun up for us
Then with Grampy you would stay,
Just you and me Callum boy
In our sunny special day.

# 60TH BIRTHDAY REFLECTIONS

Where did all those lines come from?
They weren't there yesterday,
Where did that old colour come from?
Gosh I've gone so grey.

Where did that ache come from?
It's beginning to get me down,
Still, with all these unwanted 60$^{th}$ gifts
Came a free-bus-pass into town!

*Kelvin Smith*

# CREEPY CRAWLY SPIDER

Creepy crawly spider, crawling overhead,
I can see you above me, while lying in my bed.

Creepy crawly spider, you never make a sound,
Do you realise while you're crawling, you are upside down?

Creepy crawly spider, I watch you as you crawl,
Creeping ever close to me, crawling down the wall.

Creepy crawly spider, I won't turn off the light,
I close my eyes for a second and you are out of sight.

Creepy crawly spider, my eyes are everywhere,
Open wide as I can as round the room I stare.

Creepy crawly spider, come out so I can see,
I then turn round only to find – you lying next to me!

AHHHH! Creepy crawly spider, sleeping overhead,
'Cause I'm downstairs well away from you, on the sofa bed.

# I AM HERE

I am here and you are there,
I just look and you just stare.

You can see me and I see you,
So what are we supposed to do?

There seems to be an inner fear,
We're so distant yet we're so near.

Life can sometimes be unfair,
I am here and you are there.

Kelvin Smith

# GUTS FULL

We stand around, rant and cuss,
Because progression's killing us.

Carbon emissions make us die,
As we drive our cars and fly the sky.

We admit sometimes life's a drag,
Then stand outside and smoke a fag.

One more pint, it can't hurt,
But it's slowly killing us that's a cert.

But they are the goodies – life's teasers,
And all the unfair are life's diseases.

Something will get us that's for sure,
So a guts full of teasers can kill or cure.

We've all got vices and they're growing,
But it's those vices that keep us going.

And when those vices catch my eye –
I hope to get my guts full, before I die!

# UNDER THE STARS

Under the stars I fell for you
Over the cliff and through the hue,
And when I am well, you know what I'll do?
I'll go back to that cliff and I'll take you.

Then under the stars you'll fall for me
Over that cliff and into the sea,
I'll get my revenge just wait and see
And should you survive, we're quits – agree!?

*Kelvin Smith*

# JOE

Sitting alone with nothing to do,
Except stare into space thinking of you.

What are you doing? I haven't a clue,
It's all I've asked since I lost you.

I sit by the window looking through,
Reminiscing of times I spent with you.

But you're not coming back, that much is true,
Poor old Joey – I bet a cat's had you.

# PALPITATIONS

Anxiety, panic and palpitations,
I frigging hate these sensations.

I always think I'm going to die,
Because death always seems so bloody nigh.

From the very second that they start,
I hear the beating of my heart.

Echoing loud within my head,
They'll only stop when I am dead.

My blood pumps till I feel weak,
Makes me feel like I'm a freak.

Every minute I count the beats,
Panicking and sweating between the sheets.

When they stop they leave me shattered,
My body's limp and totally battered.

Anxiety, panic and palpitations,
I frigging hate these sensations!

*Kelvin Smith*

# WHY?

Places on earth not discovered yet
Perhaps one day soon,
Cures on earth not affordable yet
So why go to the moon?

We pay for women to dance 'round poles
Then snub a beggar's sigh,
We'll buy a stranger a drink or two
Then make a loved one cry – why?

# MR CHOO

"How do you do Mr Choo,
Where are you off today?"
"Where-why-when-who?" said Mr Choo –
"I'm not prepared to say".

He walked through town as the rain lashed down
But still he raised his hat,
"Where-why-when-who?" said Mr Choo –
He's just not one for chat.

He hurried past – Choo-choo fast
Disappearing through the rain,
"Where-why-when-who?" said Mr Choo –
"To stop and talk's insane".

Kelvin Smith

# MOTHER'S DAY

They turn up with flowers
Chocolates and a card,
It's easy turning up for them
It's staying they find hard.

"I've got to rush", they say,
"Sorry can't stay long,
Happy Mother's Day Mum –
See you soon so-long".

They're rushing off somewhere else
Mustn't let others down,
Mum'll go back to her worn out chair
In her dressing gown.

She thinks kindly of them all
Popping in and out,
They'll keep in touch till she goes –
(There is the will no doubt).

Soon as they've gone she'll reminisce
Of her life and marriage,
She'll sit and stare at the daffs left there
That they just bought at the garage.

# THE OWL'S C.V.

I'm just an owl, I hoot not howl
I hunt by night like a bat,
I am a bird, so it's quite absurd
More often than not I'm sat.

I got big scary eyes – they say I'm wise
And I accept that's sound,
I sleep all day, it's just my way
Then nightly fly around.

I don't know why I rarely fly
I sleep my life away,
I just take root with the occasional hoot
There's nothing else to say.

*Kelvin Smith*

## MILLIONAIRE

To be a millionaire
Sat by there
In a golden chair
Wouldn't be fair –
Without you.

To live like a count
With a large bank account
To have that amount
Of a never ending fount –
Without you.

At last feel free
After winning the lottery
Well actually –
You didn't go halves with me –
So yes! – without you.

# NO MATTER

No matter how high you jump
You'll always come back down,
No matter how much the sun shines
It'll still make you frown.

No matter how good you are
Bad will still come your way,
And no matter how down you are
You'll be high one day.

*Kelvin Smith*

# IF I COULD

If I could dance – I'd dance,
If I could sing – I'd sing,
If I could love, I'd think about it,
If I could cry – I wouldn't stop,
If I could run – I'd fly
If I could kill – I'd die,
If I could find – I'd search,
If I could draw, then I would on my experiences,
If I could …. I probably wouldn't,
And if Jesus is listening, I did try,
And if I could have, I would have, but not always.

## AUNTY SANDY

I have to tell you about my Aunt,
Who once sat on a cactus plant.

You wouldn't think that very strange,
Except for the very noticeable change.

She now gets the needle with everyone,
She's stopped drinking water and sits in the sun.

Dressing in green clothes, that's her goal,
And changed her name to Sandy, by deed poll.

I went to water her yesterday,
But she'd gone to the Sahara on holiday.

*Kelvin Smith*

# STARDOM OR BUST

Keep it sparkling or it'll rust,
Keep on striving – stardom or bust.

You're getting older – you're turning grey,
But keep on thinking – maybe one day.

Don't be negative – no more grieving,
Gotta be positive – keep on believing.

Like everyone else – you're something rare,
Keep on searching, it's there somewhere.

The world seems such a big wide place,
Yet there is only one human race.

You may be hungry – can't afford a crust,
But follow your dreams – stardom or bust.

# HE'S WAITING THERE ....

He's still waiting there
Just sat in his chair
I don't think it's natural – is it?
It can't be fun
Waiting for someone
Just to come and visit.

We'll all get old
With no-one to hold
He's just silently sat,
A recognisable face
Would be nice in that place
Just for a comforting chat.

He misses you so
And wants you to know
Life can be so unfair,
He's got nothing to do
Except wait for you
To visit him sat in that chair.

*Kelvin Smith*

# SKIMBLE-SKAMBLE

Skimble-skamble
Met a vandal,
In a zamble on a ramble.
He tried to take my silver spangle,
Hence the tangle in the bramble.

Then Judge Campbell
High in yamble,
Said any ramble was a gamble.
I was charged with intent to strangle,
What a shamble and a scandal.

Skimble-skamble
Legal wrangle,
Because a vandal stole my spangle!
No more shall I ever ramble
Into yamble, Skimble-skamble.

*My Sister and Me*

# GRANNY SMITH

Me and my Granny Smith
On Sundays visit chapel,
She's an appealing funny Granny Smith
She's just like an apple.

She can be golden and delicious
And sometimes very hip,
She can also be rotten to the core
And gets right on my pip!

*Kelvin Smith*

# CAN'T DO IT ON MY OWN

We shuffled through the fallen leaves
Autumn was our time,
That was when I was yours
And you were surely mine.

But like the ever migrating birds
You've now also flown,
And I can't shuffle through those leaves no more
Can't do it on my own.

And like those leaves I'm falling
You're the only love I've known,
Don't think I'll ever smile again
Can't do it on my own.

# CRAP CHRISTMAS

Why hasn't Santa come this year,
Now that Mum and Dad have gone?
I don't remember being naughty
Did I do something wrong?

No-one's hung my stocking
No-one's trimmed the tree,
No-one's wrapped up presents
And left toys and sweets for me.

Perhaps there is no Santa
Perhaps there is no heaven,
Perhaps I'm being a silly boy
Now I'm fifty seven.

*Kelvin Smith*

## GOODBYE (*outro*)

You wanna know why
This is goodbye?
'Cause it's the end of the book
You silly – that's why.

I've got to go now
I've got to fly,
Take care – be good
God bless – goodbye.

Lightning Source UK Ltd.
Milton Keynes UK
UKOW04f1638280116

267316UK00002B/380/P